Sharolyn Turnbow

CARLEIGH'S CRY

THE CHILD
IN THE MIDDLE

Carleigh's Cry,
The Child in the Middle

©2020 Sharolyn Turnbow

print ISBN: 978-1-09832-704-0

ebook ISbBN: 978-1-09832-705-7

CHAPTER TWO

This book is dedicated to
all the Carleigh's in the world

Holding her breath, Carleigh looks at her mom and waits for a response. "Your dad and I are getting a divorce," Mom says, ashamed. The news gives Carleigh a bittersweet feeling. "He took all of his stuff, but you will see him soon." Carleigh thinks about what her dad did to her. He really hurt her feelings. She really doesn't know what to think at this moment.

Months go by, and her father hasn't come to see her. Carleigh's mom talks often about how he treated her and that he has a girlfriend. *A girlfriend*, Carleigh thought. She wonders if this is who Momma was fighting. The house is quiet and cold, but at least she doesn't have to hear her parents fuss and fight anymore.

One Saturday morning, Carleigh is startled by a knock at the door. "Get the door!" Mom calls. Carleigh runs to open it, and is shocked to see her father.

"Are you going to let me in?" he asks calmly. Carleigh can't move, but doesn't want to make him mad either. Slowly unlatching the screen door, she pushes it open. "I need you to pack up your stuff. You are staying with me for the weekend," Dad says with authority. She just stares at him.

"Baby, did you hear me? David! Why didn't you call me first?!" Mom shouts.

Dad responds angrily, "You're telling everyone about Mary Ann! What about you and your boyfriend? You think that I don't know!"

"Leave my house!"

"No, according to the temporary visitation order, this is my weekend." Dad grabs Carleigh and shoves her out the door. She leaves with only the clothing on her.

He starts the truck and, with a screech, they pull away. The silence is deafening. Carleigh glances up at him and wonders where they're going. It seems like a long time until they pull up to an unfamiliar house. "Don't tell your mom where I'm taking you," Dad says softly. Carleigh looks at him with disgust and doesn't say a word. As they walk to the door, a woman opens it and looks out with a grin on her face. "Carleigh, this is Mary Ann. Mary Ann, this is Carleigh."

"Hey Carleigh, it's a pleasure to meet you, sweetie." Carleigh stares at her and gives her a look of disgust.

"Carleigh, you show some respect when an adult is speaking to you!" Dad shouts.

It's an effort, but Carleigh mumbles, "Hi." Mary Ann and Dad settle down in front of the TV, but Carleigh stands at the door with her arms folded and glances around the house. She is unsure where to go and can't move.

"This baby is really kicking!" Mary Ann says, getting Carleigh's attention. Carleigh looks at her dad to hear his response. He doesn't say a word, just looks at the TV as if nothing was said. Carleigh tries to ignore Mary Ann, but glances up to find her staring. Mary Ann has a smirk on her face. Carleigh rolls her eyes and avoids looking at her.

"Dad, can I go to Grandma's?"

"Yes, we're going to leave in a minute."

"Carleigh, you can sit down," Mary Ann says.

"No, I'm fine," Carleigh says quickly. Carleigh continues to ignore her and leans against the wall. She is tired from standing.

"Let's go," her father says. "See you tonight," he says to Mary Ann.

Carleigh stamps out of the house and slams the door. She knows her father will chastise her because of her actions, but she is ready to leave. Another thirty minutes pass and she wonders, *what is he doing? I'm not going back in there. I'll wait outside!*

When Dad finally comes out, he and Mary Ann are smirking at each other.

Carleigh rolls her eyes again. *Unbelievable!!*

Dad doesn't say a word. It's a quiet ride until he turns on the radio and starts singing. She looks at him in disgust. *Do I really want to hear him sing?* As they pull up to her grandmother's house, Carleigh jumps out before the truck stops.

"What's wrong with you, girl?" Grandmother asks as Carleigh runs past her and into the house. She heads straight into the room that's been prepared for her.

"What's wrong with her?" she hears her grandmother ask.

"I don't know what's wrong. She's a crazy girl! Her mother has her all messed up!"

"Go in there and talk to her, David."

"You talk to her. If I do, I am going to hurt her." He storms out the door. Carleigh hears him leave and cautiously comes back into the living room.

"Come on out baby and talk to Grandma." Carleigh sits on the sofa and Grandma place her hand on Carleigh's shoulder. "I know that this is hard for you right now. Your parents need to get themselves together." As Grandmother talks, Carleigh's mind wanders.

Dad and Mary Ann! I can't trust anyone! Mom and Dad's divorce! Mixed feelings about her aunt! Thoughts are spinning in her head, and she hears a voice, "Carleigh! Carleigh! You hear me talking to you, girl?"

"Ma'am, what did you say?" she whispers.

"Girl, you really need Jesus." Her grandmother shakes her head as she walks into the kitchen. *Another person talking about Jesus.*

"Are you hungry?" her grandmother calls.

Approaching the kitchen, Carleigh sees that her grandmother has prepared spaghetti and vegetables. It looks and smells really good. Stirring the spaghetti, she notices something moving. It's big, black, and doesn't belong in food. *A roach*! Carleigh drops the spoon and runs into the living room.

"Are you okay, girl?"

"Yes, I'm not really hungry, Grandma. I'll get something to snack on at the store." She hurries out the door. On her return, she can hear her grandmother talking on the phone.

"Someone or something has evidently made her quite upset... I don't like her, and you can't make me like her! Where are Carleigh's clothes? You need to get yourself together! You are still married!" Carleigh walks into the bedroom and closes the door quietly.

A few minutes later, her grandmother looks in to check on her, and Carleigh puts on a smile as if she is happy to be there.

"Carleigh, you know I'm here if you want to talk, baby. Is there anything that you want to tell me?"

"No ma'am, I'm Okay. I just need to get some sleep, that's all."

The next day, Dad comes in with a big smile on his face. "Hey baby, you ready?"

Carleigh looks at him as if he is joking. Her grandmother is furious. "David, you haven't spent any time with her, and you come in like you've been here the whole time." He ignores her, and Carleigh grabs a bag and walks outside to the truck.

"Bye, Grandma. See you later!" Carleigh yells out the window.

"Did you have fun at your grandma's house?" her dad asks, looking over at her.

"It was Okay," Carleigh responds, still looking out the window. There is no more conversation on the ride back to her mom's house, the cab of the truck filled with tension. Dad stops the truck and Carleigh leaps out and runs toward the house. She doesn't say goodbye, but looks over her shoulder to see if he's left. She sighs in relief as the truck pulls out and goes into the house.

"Momma! Momma!" She is nowhere to be found, but then she hears her mom's voice coming from the back yard.

Mom is on the phone, so Carleigh waves to let her know she's home. Mom waves back and continues talking, her voice growing louder and louder.

"He can have Mary Ann! I have someone, too! I can't wait until I divorce his ass!"

Mom has a boyfriend, too? I wonder if that's who she was talking to at the hotel. Carleigh shudders, and she walks into her room to lie down.

A few minutes later, Mom walks into her room. "What's wrong?"

Carleigh stares, silent.

"Carleigh!"

"Nothing, just tired momma!" she answers quickly.

"Why are you looking at me that way, girl? What'd you do at your dad's house?" The next words are mumbled, "He was probably with that woman."

Carleigh ignores her comment and answers, "It was okay, just different."

"You'll be going there every other weekend." Seeing the look of horror cross Carleigh's face, her mom adds, "Ask him if you could bring a friend with you."

"Okay, Momma. That would make it better! I'll ask London if she wants to go next time."

"Carleigh, when you go over there, I need you to do something for me. Your dad took a couple of items and I need you to get them for me."

Carleigh gapes at her mom. "What Momma? I can't take anything from over there! Dad would know, and he'd be really mad."

"What did I say? These things are important! I'll let you know what I need before you go back."

Carleigh bites her lip as Mom leaves the room. *What could mom possibly want of Dad's? How do I know where to find it? Is it at Grandma's or Mary Ann's?* She wants to talk to Mom about her encounter with Mary Ann, but knows it would only make things worse between her parents. *I hope Mom forgets,* she thinks, and feels less anxious with the thought.

"Carleigh, there's some boy here for you!" Mom yells down the hallway.

Who in the world could it be? Oh! It's William! Carleigh feels little butterflies in her stomach, but keeps a serious face.

"What are you doing here, boy?"

"Do I need to leave?" William asks apologetically.

"I'm sorry William. I'm just tired."

"Where have you been, Carleigh?"

How does he know I haven't been home? "I've been at my grandma's house. Why? And how did you know I was gone?"

"Dang, Carleigh what's up with all these questions?"

"I was just asking, William," Carleigh giggles. "I have to go to my Grandma's house every other weekend now."

"Yeah, I know how that goes," William says, looking down at his shoes.

Carleigh was about to ask what he meant, but decides to ignore that statement. "I hope London will come over there with me next time."

"You think that I could come over there with ya'll?" William asked.

"Heck, no! My dad would kill you!" Carleigh sees the sincerity in William's face.

"I was just going to stop by," he says, looking embarrassed.

"We'll see, okay?"

"I just want to be your friend, Carleigh." For some odd reason, Carleigh feels differently around William than she did with Michael. She doesn't feel pressured when she's with William.

"I really need to get some rest. I'll talk to you later."

"Yeah, okay. But don't forget to call me when you and London are at your grandmother's," he says, as he turns to leave.

. . . .

Two weeks later, Carleigh is back at her grandmother's house, on another visit with her dad. This time, London was allowed to be there for company.

"London, I'm so glad you are here with me! It's so boring by myself."

"Baby, can you come here for a minute?" her dad calls from the other room.

"Yes, Dad."

"You know, when you come over here you can't have someone with you all the time. This is our time together," he says.

Hell, you aren't even here, she thinks to herself. "Okay, Dad," she says softly and walks back into her room, where London is waiting. When Carleigh hears her dad's truck leave, she just shakes her head and focuses on London.

"What did your dad want?"

"Nothing. He just wanted to make sure that we didn't need anything," Carleigh hoped that London didn't hear what her father had said.

"Oh, okay. Let's go to the store and get some snacks."

As they head for the door, Grandmother is cooking. "Hey girls, are you all hungry?"

Carleigh shudders as the thought of the roach that she found in the spaghetti crosses her mind. "No, Grandma we are going to just walk up to the store and get something to eat."

"Ya'll need to eat something. That's not real food," Carleigh's grandmother yells as they walk out.

"Have you been talking to William?" London asks, giggling.

"Yeah," Carleigh giggles softly.

"Girl, what have ya'll been talking about?" London asks, tugging on Carleigh's arm.

"Okay, okay. Dang, I was going to tell you when I got a chance! Anyways, he came over to my house, we talked, and …" Carleigh hesitated.

"What did he say?" London asks.

"William wants to come over here!" Carleigh says quickly. London starts jumping up and down as if she had won the lottery. "London! It's not like that!" Carleigh is nervous. She wants London to think she has everything under control.

The rest of the day passes with Carleigh and London laughing and playing. As night approaches, Grandmother goes to bed.

"Carleigh, let's call William. Let's see if he can come over."

Carleigh's heart begins to race. She can't come up with the words to respond to London.

"Carleigh, you hear me?" London shakes Carleigh to get her attention.

"London, he is not going to come." Carleigh says, hoping London will leave the idea alone.

"Girl, didn't he ask you if he could come over?"

"Yes, but I don't think he was serious."

"Well, let's see how serious he is, Carleigh!"

Fingers shaking, Carleigh calls William and he answers on the first ring. She jumps at hearing his voice and shoves the phone at London. Excitedly, London tells William that Carleigh wants to see him. London giggles, and then shoves the phone back to Carleigh. "He wants to talk to you," she whispers loudly.

"Hey, William," Carleigh says shyly. "Do you want to come over and hang with us?"

"Yes!" William shouts.

"Well, you'll have to knock on my bedroom window. I'll let you in." She hangs up the phone and the girls start giggling again.

"Girl!!! How are we going to get William in here?" London says mischievously.

"Girl!!! I don't know," Carleigh responds nervously.

"Okay, when William knocks on the window, you go to the back door and let him in. Make sure you open the door quietly. You don't want to wake your grandma."

"Naw, I will go outside and wait for him. When he arrives, I will sneak him in the house."

"Yeah, that sounds good!" They look at each other, smiling and giggling. Soon, Carleigh tiptoes out the door. Once outside, she checks out the backyard to see if William has arrived, but there's no sign of him. As she walks around, her thoughts wander. *What if Grandma wakes up? What if William wants a kiss? I hope London doesn't embarrass me.*

"Hey, Carleigh," William says softly.

She jumps, turns around, and says, embarrassed, "Hey, William."

"Are you okay about me coming over?"

"Yeah, I'm okay, let's go inside." As they walk toward the door, Carleigh's heart is racing, her thoughts scattered.

"You know, we don't have to go in, Carleigh."

With sudden relief, Carleigh remembers that London is waiting for them. "No, I'm okay." She opens the door quietly and they walk in. As they get closer to the bedroom, Carleigh sees London with her hand over her mouth.

"Hey William, I thought you weren't going to show up," she greets him quietly. "I should have known you were coming because Carleigh is here."

Sternly, Carleigh gives London a quick look in an effort to quiet her. London stops talking and gestures Carleigh to say something. A light from under the door catches Carleigh's eye, but Carleigh hasn't said a word.

London murmurs softly, "What's wrong, Carleigh?" Carleigh motions for London and William to be quiet, then she hears a car door slamming. The back door opens and slams against the wall. Carleigh gestures wildly for London to open the window so William can run. As William jumps out the window, Carleigh and London jump into bed.

Dad bursts into the room and notices the open window, then stamps out to go outside. Carleigh and London look at each other, afraid that Dad will catch William outside. Carleigh whispers, "Girl, I can't believe my Dad is here tonight."

"I hope William doesn't get caught." The back door slams closed, and they hear Dad sit down on the living room couch and turn on the TV. Thinking they're in the clear, Carleigh and London finally drift off to sleep.

"Get your asses up!" Dad roars, waking Carleigh and London, who jump out of bed and rush to the living room. "You think I don't know that you had someone here!" The girls remain silent. "Once I find out who was here, I'm going to beat his ass and yours, too!"

Carleigh tries to explain, but Dad keeps cutting her off. Grandma enters the room and asks in amazement, "David, what's going on?"

"These two fools are sitting here looking all innocent, but I know they had someone here last night."

"David, as far as I know there was no one here."

Dad keeps yelling, demanding to know who was there, but Carleigh and London stay quiet. "Get your stuff, I'm taking you home." The girls return to the bedroom, where Carleigh looks at London in embarrassment.

London puts her hand on Carleigh's shoulder. "Everything will be okay," she whispers.

"Get moving!" Dad shouts. Carleigh and London head toward Dad's truck, and Carleigh is too embarrassed to say anything to her grandmother. As they drive across town, no one says a word. When they arrive, the girls jump out and Dad speeds off. Mom is surprised to see them.

"What's wrong?"

"I'm never going back over there!" Carleigh states and walks in the house.

Mom bites her lip, then says, "London, call your mom. It's time for you to go home, sweetie." London leaves soon after, and Mom approaches Carleigh about her visit with her dad. Carleigh refuses to answer.

"Since you won't tell me what happened, did you get that stuff I asked you to get?"

"Yes, Momma. It's right here." Mom grabs the items excitedly and leaves the room. "That's all she cares about," Carleigh says aloud in disgust. She lays on her bed confused, unsure what to think. She picks up the phone to call William, but slams it down again. The situation is running around in her head. She decides to get up and overhears mom on the phone.

"Carleigh came home mad as hell," she hears her mom whisper. "I bet her dad was mean to her." Carleigh shakes her head and goes outside.

Carleigh sits on the front porch deep in thought. *Should I go back and visit Dad? He just drops in whenever he feels like it.*"

She doesn't have long to think about it, because she sees William walking toward the house. *Oh my God! No!*" she thinks in fear. She runs to the back of the house in hopes that William hasn't seen her.

"Carleigh! Carleigh!" Mom shouts from the front door, but Carleigh is hiding from William. After what seems like hours, Carleigh walks back to the front of the house. She'll have to face William one day, and admits to herself *it would've been perfect if London wasn't around.* As she reaches the porch, she is shocked. William is sitting there! He grabs her and hugs her tightly. She doesn't know how to feel and keeps her arms to her side.

"Girl, I've been worried about you," William says with concern. Carleigh gapes at William, speechless. "What's wrong, Carleigh? I'm trying to be your friend!"

"I'm okay, William," she says softly.

"Do I look okay, Carleigh?" William stares into Carleigh's eyes. "I hid under your grandma's house until your dad went back in the house. Don't worry, he didn't see me." She finally looks up at William and smiles with relief. Mom has been watching them the whole time.

"Carleigh, get in here! Where have you been, girl?" she shouts angrily.

"Talk to you later," William says as he walks away.

"I didn't hear you, Mom," Carleigh responds. She grins to herself as she thinks about William. Mom notices and asks if she likes him. "Because I don't like him. Why's he's coming over here all of a sudden? Do we know his family? You better be careful because boys only want one thing," Mom goes on and on. Carleigh can only think about how William made her feel. It's a new feeling, and it scared her. Carleigh's heart is beating hard. She tries to think of other things to suppress her true feelings.

"I'm not going back to visit Dad!" Carleigh says aloud.

"What did you say?"

Carleigh decides to say something she knew her mom would like. "I'm not going to Grandma's house anymore. Dad was being mean," Carleigh says boldly.

"And you don't have to go back either!" her mom says firmly.

Later that night, while she's getting ready for bed, she hears Mom whispering on the phone. "I told you he was being mean to her.

"She doesn't want to go back over there and I'm not going to make her." Carleigh smirks to herself. She knows she doesn't have to go back. It's music to her ears. *Let's see how Dad likes that!* Carleigh thinks to herself. *On the other hand, what if he gets so mad that he comes over here and fights with Mom?* She has mixed feelings, but reassures herself. Mom knows what to do.

. . . .

Walking into school on Monday, Carleigh is approached by London and several other girls. "Hey Carleigh! Let's go eat breakfast!" London doesn't say anything about what happened and neither does Carleigh. As the group walks into the cafeteria, they are approached by an older group of girls.

"Look at all those virgins!" The older girls start laughing.

"We're not virgins!" Carleigh and her friends respond. *How cool would it be to have had sex before?* Carleigh wonders. Then she wonders if her friends have had sex for real or not.

"There you go daydreaming again, girl!" London says. Carleigh is embarrassed because the girls are staring at her. She walks to the line and picks up a tray. She could feel the girls still looking at her in concern.

"Are you okay, girl?" London whispers.

"I'm okay, London" Carleigh says without looking at her.

"You know I was just playing with you."

"Yeah, I know," Carleigh replies.

"We can talk later," London says as she walks back to the other girls. As they all sit down and start eating, the conversation turns to sex. Someone asks, "Who has done it before?" Carleigh's heart stops. A few of the girls confide they've done it before and how good it felt. "What about you guys?" One of the girls asks Carleigh and London.

"Yeah, we've done it before," London says instantly. Carleigh listens as London carries on. She knows London is lying for them. *Or is she lying for me?* Carleigh thinks to herself. She wonders if London has done it or not. The conversation continues as the girls talk about their experiences.

Carleigh is scared, and her mind wonders. London lightly touches Carleigh's knee as if she knows. The other girls leave the table, and Carleigh can't wait to ask London if she has done it before, but London has read Carleigh's mind. "No, Carleigh I haven't done it yet. I know, though, who I'm going to do it with."

"Who?"

"My boyfriend, Larry!" London says excitedly.

"Who is Larry?" Carleigh says attentively.

"You don't know him" London responds nonchalantly.

"You should do it with William or maybe Michael? You know he likes you, too."

Carleigh freezes. She can't imagine losing her virginity to Michael. As for William, she barely knows him and has only recently started seeing him as a friend. *Get it together,* Carleigh thinks to herself. *London seems so happy with her decision.* "When are you going to do it, London?"

"I don't know, but it's going to be soon." Carleigh stares speechlessly at London. "I'll tell you when it happens, Girl. Don't worry." Now Carleigh's heart beats faster than ever.

The thought of having sex makes her nervous. "Girl let's get to class," London says.

On the way to class, Carleigh and London laugh and talk with friends, but the whole time Carleigh tries to suppress her feelings. *If London is going to do it soon, I know I will have to do it.* As they approach the classroom, Carleigh sees William. He is distracted by one of his friends and doesn't see her. Then Carleigh glances at London. She's occupied and doesn't see William, either. Carleigh is glad to know London hasn't seen him. Mrs. Bostick gives Carleigh a strange look as they walk in. Carleigh gives her an unpleasant look back.

"Lil Miss Carleigh, do you have a problem?" Mrs. Bostick says, loudly enough for everyone to hear. Conversations trail off as everyone stares at Carleigh. Carleigh takes a deep breath and thinks to herself. *Now, I could tell everybody what I heard her say about me! I thought I could trust her nosey ass, but she is just like the rest of these gossipers! What about this child of God stuff she said to me?*

"Did you hear me, girl?" Mrs. Bostick repeats firmly. Carleigh jumps and says nothing. Her classmates whisper to each other, trying to figure out what's going on. Carleigh sits at her desk embarrassed. It's a long day. Her classmates continue to stare, and Ms. Bostick is cutting eyes at her. Carleigh finally goes to the bathroom, desperate to escape. She thinks of her humiliation and how it made her feel. She listens as girls go in and out. She decides to go back to class. The bell rings as she slowly walks back. *Class is over,* Carleigh thinks. She runs into the room, grabs her things, and hurriedly leaves. Mrs. Bostick doesn't say a word, just stares.

"Wait up!" William yells.

Dang, I was hoping he wouldn't see me, Carleigh thinks to herself. She keeps walking, pretending she doesn't hear him.

"Carleigh, I know you hear me!" William cries, running after her, but Carleigh continues walking.

Finally, William grabs her arm and Carleigh pulls her arm away. William stares as he takes a step back. "What's wrong with you?"

"I want to be left alone!" Carleigh sobs out, but keeps walking, not looking back at William or seeing anyone or anything around her. She's furious with Mrs. Bostick's treatment and how London embarrassed her. *I'm glad that this is my last year at that school. I won't have to see Ms. Bostick and those teachers again!* As Carleigh gets closer to home, she thinks about Cece. She really misses him and wishes he didn't live so far away. *Now, I know why he stays away,* Carleigh says to herself.

The years pass and Carleigh enters high school. Carleigh is overwhelmed with all of the older students, especially the older boys. They are all paying close attention to her. "Spissssss … Spisssss …" was all she could hear as she walked, hoping to find a familiar face. Carleigh stared straight ahead as if she can't hear anything. *OMG, where is London? I am so nervous!* Carleigh was unsure about how long she could keep her composure, but she was enjoying the attention to some degree.

Finally, Carleigh was able to see her classmates in an area separate from the upperclassmen. With a sigh of relief, she walked up to them. "Hey y'all! Man, is this crazy or what?" Carleigh says. Her friends agree, and are clearly just as nervous as Carleigh. Carleigh looks around to see London and an unfamiliar boy.

"Carleigh, this is my boyfriend, Larry," London says giddily. Larry is an upperclassman. Carleigh's thoughts turn to what London said about having sex with Larry. Larry looks uncomfortable with London showing him off. Everyone looks shocked to know that London is dating an older boy. "Come walk with us, Carleigh," London says. As they walk down the hallway, Larry whispers something in London's ear. London shakes her head no. Carleigh ignores them and keeps walking as if she is paying attention to something else.

"Do you have a boyfriend, Carleigh?" Larry asks with a little smirk on his face.

"No," Carleigh says, embarrassed.

"Well, I have a friend named Torey that would be interested in you."

"Yes, she would love to meet him," London interrupts.

Carleigh is too embarrassed to respond. As they continue down the hallway, Torey is on Carleigh's mind. *How could he be interested in me?* Carleigh thinks. Coming out of her thoughts, Carleigh sees London kiss Larry goodbye before they walk into the classroom.

"Girl, isn't Larry cute and fine?" London says while tightly squeezing Carleigh's hand.

"He's cute," Carleigh quietly responds.

"Girl, what's wrong? Aren't you ready to meet Torey?" Before Carleigh could answer, the teacher starts making announcements. London whispers, "We'll talk." As Carleigh and London walk out after class, Larry approaches.

"Carleigh, I told Torey about you," he says briefly.

"Oh, okay," were the only words she could think to say.

"Tell him to call her," London says. Carleigh glares at London.

"He'll have to call you when he gets out of class," Larry says as he pulls London closer to him. Carleigh doesn't respond. Waving goodbye, she heads to her next class. Walking slowly there are many thoughts going through her head. *Who is Torey? How could he possibly be interested in me? Do I know him* Music class gives her a little sense of relief from all her thoughts.

Finally, it's the end of the day. Carleigh notices flyers posted throughout the school about a back-to-school party as she rushes out to catch the bus. Entering the bus, she is approached by friends about the back to school party. *I wish they would leave me alone already!* she thinks angrily, but simply smiles. "Yes, I'm going." Everyone else gathers in the back of the bus, while she decides to stay close to the front and away from the noise. It's a relief when no one comes to the front, pressuring her to join them. She passes Dad's job, but there's no one there. Her thoughts turn to Dad. She is both sad and mad at the same time. *He doesn't love me! How could he do this to our family! I don't want to ever see him again! If I look straight ahead, I can pretend he doesn't exist.*

Mom is waiting by the car when Carleigh gets off the bus. "Come on, we're going to get your child support from your dad."

"Huh!? Mom, Dad is not there," she says quickly.

"Yes, he is. Let's go!" They drive back the way they came and park across the street from his job. Carleigh is instructed to go in and pick up the thirty-five dollars from her dad. Carleigh goes in, but her dad is nowhere to be found. She heads out to give Mom the news.

"That bastard!" her mom says angrily. "He can't even pay me what he owes me! Don't worry we will be back!" She rants on and on.

"Mom, do I have to go back?" Carleigh asks, irritated.

"Yes, I need the money!"

"Where are we going mom?"

"Hush, girl, you'll see,"

As they drive, the houses look familiar to Carleigh. Mary Ann's street and home are not far. Mom passes the street and looks in that direction, but keeps driving. Then she suddenly stops and turns the car around.

When Carleigh looks up, they are at Mary Ann's house, and Mom tells Carleigh to knock on the door. She looks at Mom in fear when she sees Dad's truck, then remembers that Mom is unaware Carleigh has been here before.

"Mom, who lives here?"

"Girl, do what I tell you!" her mom says. Carleigh slowly gets out of the car and walks towards the door. "Go on!" her mom shouts from her car window. She takes one step at a time until she reaches the door. The door is closed and there seems to be no movement inside. Carleigh knocks softly. "Knock harder than that, Girl!" her mom shouts.

Carleigh knocks a little harder in hopes no one would come to the door. *I can't believe Mom has me knocking at this door.* Carleigh's heart is pounding faster and faster with each knock. Luckily, no one comes to the door. "Come on, Girl, I know they're in there" her mom says as Carleigh runs back to the car. Carleigh looks at her mom in disgust. She couldn't believe that her mom had her do that. Carleigh and her mom don't say anything on the way home. Carleigh could tell that her mom was furious. She wanted to ask if she could go to the party, but she was too upset. She decides to wait.

By the end of the week, everyone is excited about the back-to-school party. This would be London and Carleigh's first high school party, and they can't stop talking about it. London was all about Larry this and Larry that. There was no talk about Torey and that was okay with Carleigh. She just enjoyed getting away from home every chance she could. The party was packed with students, everyone dancing and mingling. London went immediately to search for Larry.

Carleigh walked around to scope out the party. As she walked through the crowd, she could feel people touching her, trying to get her attention. Carleigh never looked back to see who it was. She found some people she knew and started dancing with them. She danced and danced until London grabbed Carleigh's hand. London maneuvers them through the crowd toward Larry, who is sitting with another guy. He is older and very handsome.

"This is Torey, Carleigh," London says happily. *OMG! He's here!* Carleigh nervously says to herself. Carleigh moves closer to London and asks her to say it again, acting as if she can't hear because of the music. "This is Torey," London repeats, giving Carleigh time to get her thoughts together. She looks at Torey and blushes. Torey stays seated and looks Carleigh up and down as if drawing her with his eyes. "Go over there and say something," London says, pushing her toward him.

"Hey, how are you?" Carleigh says, reaching out her hand to him. Standing up, Torey rises and gives Carleigh a hug. She melts into Torey arms. He smells so good. Carleigh closes her eyes and savors the feel of his strong arms wrapped around her. It was as secure as a father makes a daughter.

"Okay, that's enough!" London giggles. Torey makes eye contact with Larry and nods his head. Larry smiles and whispers to London.

"Come here, baby, and sit on my lap," Torey says to Carleigh. She's curious about why Torey is so interested in her, but she does as he asks. "How are you liking high school?" Torey whispers in her ear.

"It's good," Carleigh says shyly. "What high school do you go to?"

"High school? I'm in college, sweetheart," Torey says, smiling and trying not to laugh. Carleigh turns her face and tries to remain calm. She wants to scream for help. "You okay?" he asks in concern.

"I'm okay, I just can't talk for this loud music," Carleigh replies without making eye contact. She feels out of place and scared. *There is no way that he could be interested in me.*

"I've been watching you for some time now. You have always been pretty to me, Carleigh," Torey says in a sincere voice. "I want to take care of you," he continues.

Carleigh feels butterflies in her stomach. Torey makes her feel special. She begins to feel comfortable enough to look at Torey directly. Focusing, she notices his teeth are the best-looking teeth she has ever seen. He's muscular, and has exceptionally smooth-looking skin. It looked like he was an athlete or maybe worked out a lot.

Carleigh and Torey talked and talked until the dance was over. Walking out, they held hands. "I just want you to know that you are going to be my girl," Torey says.

"Okay," Carleigh says blushing. Once she gets home, Carleigh can't sleep. She is amazed about how the night turned out and how Torey makes her feel. She felt special, like she was the luckiest girl in the world. Carleigh felt like she was in love.

Soon, Carleigh and Torey are inseparable. They discover many similarities and get along very well. Torey came home on breaks to see Carleigh. Her classmates know she is dating

Torey. She didn't realize how popular Torey was until she was approached by one of her classmates with some startling news about Torey. Her classmate pulls her aside and finds a proper place for them to talk. "What's up?" Carleigh asks with a puzzled look.

"I want you to please listen to me." the girl says. "How well do you know Torey?" Carleigh stares at her, unsure of how to answer the question while the girl continues. "Well, Torey is bad news! He and my sister were dating, and he use to physically abuse her."

Carleigh's heart drops. She doesn't want to believe what she has heard. *Torey is not like that! Torey is too sweet to me!* Coming out of her thoughts, Carleigh looks at the girl and accuses, "You're just jealous because he likes me! Torey said that people would start spreading lies about him!" The girl walks away, looking at Carleigh in disbelief. Carleigh feels good about standing up for Torey, but at the same time, has mixed feelings about what the girl said.

At the end of the day, she calls Torey on the phone. Carleigh immediately tells him about what her classmate told her. Torey does not respond. Startled by his silence, Carleigh asks him, "Are you ok?"

"I'm just tired of people lying about me, that's all." Torey says nonchalantly. "You don't believe her, do you?"

"No, baby!" Carleigh says instantly.

"You're with me, right?" asks Torey.

"You know I'm with you!" "I'll be home soon to see you. You know we've been together for some months now, and I think it's time for you to give me something…"